GOD'S PROMISE OF PROTECTION

A BIBLE STUDY & DEVOTIONAL ON PSALM 91

BUSHY PARK NAZARENE

God's Promise of Protection "A Bible Study & Devotional on Psalm 91"
Copyright ©2022 by Bushy Park Nazarene
ISBN: 978-976-96765-8-9

Unless otherwise noted, all scripture quotations are from the New King James Version of the Bible. Copyright © 1982 by Thomas Nelson, Inc. Used by permission. All rights reserved.

Cover Photo 1 by: Amanda Carden from Shutterstock.com
Cover Photo 2 by: FatCamera from GettyImages.com

Cover Design: ThinkBigGraphics
Telephone: Whatsapp/Call: 823-8970
Email: thinkbiggraphics246@gmail.com
Instagram: thinkbiggraphicsbds

SHELEV PUBLISHING
"Where Passion, Purpose and Publishing Collide"
www.shelevpublishing.com
Email: Shelevpublishing@outlook.com
Instagram: ShelevPublishing
Telephone: 1 (246) 257-9611

This Book Belongs to:

_____

HOW TO USE THIS BOOK

This book is split into two: the first part being a Bible Study, and the second part a Devotional. The Bible study section contains contributions from some of the members of Bushy Park Nazarene.

Bible Study:

Get your Bible, notebook, highlighters, pen and a concordance. For those who prefer technology, you can use your device.

It is best to read the surrounding verses for context before we go through verse by verse. So, read Psalm 91 about three times.

Open with a word of prayer and ask Holy Spirit for the revelation.

As you examine each verse, make a note of the words that stand out to you and highlight them.

Ask yourself the five W's: Who, Why, What, Where and When. See some examples below:

> Who is the writer? Example: (The Apostle Paul)
> Who was the text written to? Example: (The Ephesians)
> What type of literature is it? (Historical, prophetic, or part of an **epistle,** etc)

Getting the meaning of these words in Hebrew/ Greek can change the way you see things helps give you clarity and context. Use your concordance to research the words you highlighted.

Read the verse you're studying in different translations and note any new understanding you receive.

The Bible was written for us but not to us, so try to understand how the text applied to the people it was written to. What did the verse mean at the time it was written?

The Bible talks about being hearers of the word and not doers. To ensure you do both, apply the scripture to your life. You have gained the knowledge, but you must make the application.

Devotional:

Open with a word of prayer. Holy Spirit is the revealer of truth, so ask Him to do just that as you read for encouragement.

Take the time to answer the questions honestly in each devotional. Being open and honest can bring healing and growth. See it as your personal safe space.

Add your prayer for the day and ask God for strength to live out what you would have read.

Take the time to write and declare some things over your life pertaining to the topic.

Psalm 91

1 He who dwells in the secret place of the Most High
Shall abide under the shadow of the Almighty.

2 I will say of the Lord, "He is my refuge and my fortress;
My God, in Him I will trust."

3 Surely, He shall deliver you from the snare of the fowler
And from the perilous pestilence.

4 He shall cover you with His feathers,
And under His wings you shall take refuge;
His truth shall be your shield and buckler.

5 You shall not be afraid of the terror by night,
Nor of the arrow that flies by day,

6 Nor of the pestilence that walks in darkness,
Nor of the destruction that lays waste at noonday.

7 A thousand may fall at your side,
And ten thousand at your right hand;
But it shall not come near you.

8 Only with your eyes shall you look,
And see the reward of the wicked.

9 Because you have made the Lord, who is my refuge,
Even the Most High, your dwelling place,

10 No evil shall befall you,
Nor shall any plague come near your dwelling;

11 For He shall give His angels charge over you,
To keep you in all your ways.

12 In their hands they shall bear you up,
Lest you dash your foot against a stone.

13 You shall tread upon the lion and the cobra,
The young lion and the serpent you shall trample underfoot.

14 "Because he has set his love upon Me, therefore I will deliver
him; I will set him on high, because he has known My name.

15 He shall call upon Me, and I will answer him;
I will be with him in trouble; I will deliver him and honor him.

16 With long life I will satisfy him,
And show him My salvation."

Inductive BIBLE STUDY

VERSE 1

He who dwells in the secret place of the Most High Shall abide under the shadow of the Almighty.

When I think about this verse, I am immediately brought to the centrality of it in the rest of the chapter. The writer begins with an opening phrase that almost sounds like a dare to the reader. He begins, *"He who dwells in the secret place of the Most High."* This phrase made me ask myself some questions. If this secret place is hidden, does it mean that everyone cannot find it? Am I dwelling? Where is this secret place? How does one get there? And after I get there, how do I stay there? Before we go any further into the psalm, we must reflect on this phrase, as it is the basis of this chapter.

The second part continues, *"...Shall abide under the shadow of the Almighty."* This presents the imagery of a shadow. A shadow is often that which falls behind or in front of a person, object or thing. However, what is critical to take away is 'proximity'. Because a person's shadow is seen directly in front or behind them, to be in someone's shadow means you must be close enough. Therefore, when the psalmist says we will abide under the shadow, he is reminding us to (be in proximity), to the Most High. **-Pastor Gershon Forde**

The psalmist clearly states that if I dwell in the secret place of the Most High; if I place my trust, hope, love, faith and life in Christ Jesus, I will be protected under the shadow of the Father. It means I will have to decide to be in a committed relationship with the Almighty God. Which means obeying His commands, laws, precepts and doing His will. Therefore, as my protector, He will keep me under His love. However, this will only happen when I fully submit to Him. **-Minister Maria Barrow**

When I read this verse, a mother and her chicks come to mind. The chicks know fully that in the shadow of their mother they are secure. In addition, they know that under her wings is their secret place. Just as the chicks know where their secret place is, we who represent the name of Jesus should abide daily under the shadow of the Almighty and find the secret place. **-Mayleen Gittens**

He who dwells in the safety of the all-powerful God will find peace and a great measure of protection. Abiding suggests that there is consistent closeness with the Lord. This closeness only happens by being in constant communication with Him through prayer, praise, and the word. The word *"shadow"* suggests that there has to be a closeness, as a shadow reflects oneself. Resting in the shadow of the Almighty shows we are close enough to be completely protected by the Lord. **-Sonia Griffith**

God has a secret place where He abides, and it should be our aim to find it. 'Seek and ye shall find'. The protection the psalmist talks about is only for those who abide. So, if we are not close enough, that shadow cannot cover us. **-Beverly Toppin**

Being in the secret place is a glowing testimony and security for those who place their trust in God. It is an assurance for those who worship God. **-Rosalie Weekes**

The secret place the psalmist talks about is accessible to all believers, but only a few take advantage of this great opportunity. When I was a child, my friends and I would play a game where we would try to get underneath each other's shadow. This was a hard task because we had to be very close to the person who was creating the shadow. The Lord wants us to get close to Him and be under His shadow. In order to hear a secret, we have to be close to the person telling it. So, when we draw near to God, He will reveal His secrets to us. Revelation comes from intimacy. The shadow of the Almighty speaks of His protection, guidance, and security. When we pray and continuously abide in the Lord's presence, He promises us His power and guidance. We will see the goodness of God when we dwell in the secret place of the Most High. **-Ricardo Gittens**

The psalmist spoke of God as the dwelling place of His people. He is the habitation, the home of man. In Him, one can find complete security. However, many Christians only run there in their times of trouble. Instead of seeing this place as a second option, it needs to be where we habitually reside. The shadow of the Almighty shows a great nearness; therefore, we must walk very close if we want His shadow to fall on us. **-Randolph Franklin**

This psalm, and especially this verse, brought an awareness of what was lacking in my Christian walk. I knew when I was in the presence of God and when I had left. I had not yet accomplished dwelling there consistently. Studying this psalm and diving into the concept of dwelling helped me find identity, favor, protection, and provision. **-Harriette Williams**

Inductive
BIBLE STUDY

Verse 1:

_____

_____

_____

_____

_____

Examine the verse and make a note of
the words that stand out to you.

Use your concordance to research the words you highlighted and write their meaning.

_____

_____

_____

_____

Read the verse you're studying in alternate translations. Have you received any new understanding?

_____

_____

_____

_____

_____

_____

What did the verse mean at the time it was written?

_____

_____

_____

_____

_____

What other scripture/scriptures in the Bible can support this verse?

_____

_____

_____

_____

_____

How can this verse apply to your life?

_____

_____

_____

_____

_____

_____

Additional thoughts?

_____

_____

_____

_____

_____

VERSE 2

I will say of the Lord, "He is my refuge and my fortress; my God, in Him I will trust."

Verse 2 switches from the psalmist speaking about God to the psalmist giving his personal testimony. He says, *"I will say of the Lord…"* He boldly declares that the Lord is his refuge and fortress. Three times in the sentence we see the word *'my'*, which represents possession. The writer is establishing that God is personal to Him. The Lord is not just some external force that others speak about. He is a personal refuge and fortress in a time of need. And because he knows the Lord in this intimate way, the psalmist declares that he will trust in Him.

A refuge is a place where the embattled and oppressed run for hiding and safety, and a fortress is a supposedly impenetrable place. The psalmist here affirms that he will find rest in God who is both a safe and unbreachable space. The Lord is his ultimate protector. **-Pastor Gershon Forde**

This verse gives me such an assurance that as I continue in God's will, obeying His purposes in my life; I can confidently say He is my refuge. I can find peace in His presence and safety in His arms. He is always near, and I can trust Him even when I can't trust others. **-Minister Maria Barrow**

When you look at the relationship between a mother and her chicks, you can see how much they trust her. Similarly, we can completely trust God to be our refuge and fortress because He will never fail us. **-Mayleen Gittens**

Because I am dwelling in God, I can boldly affirm like the psalmist that my trust is in Him. God being my refuge means He is my hiding place, and I can run to Him whenever I feel afraid. He will deliver me from whatever harm (known and unknown) that may come. Christians are not immune to trials and temptations, but when they call upon the name of the Lord, they shall be protected. **-Sonia Griffith**

He who lives a life of intimacy with God knows the lengths of His protection. The Lord Himself becomes like a mighty refuge and fortress for them, and they abide under His protection, comfort, and care. **-Randolph Franklin**

This is a personal statement and one of such confidence. We can boldly stand on the fact that God is our strong tower. **-Beverly Toppin**

Inductive
BIBLE STUDY

Verse 2:

_____

_____

_____

_____

_____

Examine the verse and make a note of
the words that stand out to you.

Use your concordance to research the words you highlighted and write their meaning.

Read the verse you're studying in alternate translations. Have you received any new understanding?

What did the verse mean at the time it was written?

_____

_____

_____

_____

_____

What other scripture/scriptures in the Bible can support this verse?

_____

_____

_____

_____

_____

How can this verse apply to your life?

_____

_____

_____

_____

_____

_____

Additional thoughts?

_____

_____

_____

_____

_____

VERSE 3

Surely He shall deliver you from the snare of the fowler and from the perilous pestilence.

This verse begins with one of my favorite words in the Bible: *'Surely'*. This word is used to emphasize the speaker's firm belief. He declares, *"Surely He…"* This "He" refers to God, the Most High.

The psalmist declares his confidence in the God that delivers. The promise is that once we are dwelling, God will deliver us from the snare of the fowler (the traps and trapdoors that the enemy sets for us to fall), and the noisome pestilence (the frustrations and turmoil the enemy causes.) I am eternally encouraged by the beginning of the sentence, "Surely He shall", and I encourage you to take refuge in the same. **-Pastor Gershon Forde**

As I live my life as a believer, trusting the Lord and continuing to do His will, He shall deliver me from my enemies, and protect me from those who want to destroy me. He will also protect me from all kinds of diseases that would want to contaminate my body. **-Minister Maria Barrow**

Do you see how baby chicks walk around confidently with their mother? They stick close by, with their head high in the air, knowing that she will protect them from any harm. If anyone tries to attack them, mummy hen would charge at the enemy and deliver her chicks. Similarly, our Heavenly Father will interrupt all the plans of the enemy and surely deliver us. **-Mayleen Gittens**

Inductive
BIBLE STUDY

Verse 3:

_____

_____

_____

_____

_____

Examine the verse and make a note of
the words that stand out to you.

Use your concordance to research the words you highlighted and write their meaning.

_____

_____

_____

_____

Read the verse you're studying in alternate translations. Have you received any new understanding?

_____

_____

_____

_____

_____

What did the verse mean at the time it was written?

_____

_____

_____

_____

_____

What other scripture/scriptures in the Bible can support this verse?

_____

_____

_____

_____

_____

How can this verse apply to your life?

_____

_____

_____

_____

_____

_____

Additional thoughts?

_____

_____

_____

_____

VERSE 4

*He shall cover you with His feathers, and under His wings you
shall take refuge; His truth shall be your shield and buckler.*

"He shall…". These words are the beginning of a series of verses that
list out many promises the children of God can claim. The psalmist
wants us to understand that God is like a mother who watches over
her children and is always close. She will never sit idly by and watch
them being attacked. He suggests God has promised to do the same
thing for us as long as we stay in His dwelling. I hope you see
everything goes back to 'dwelling'.

The psalmist also declares that God's truth will be our shield and
buckler. When I think of these two terms, I'm immediately reminded
of battle armor. In war, one needs a shield to protect oneself from
the enemy. The buckler is also a smaller shield which is used in hand-
to-hand combat to protect against swords. The Lord wants us to
know that by dwelling in Him, we can use His truth as our defense
against all the enemy's attacks, whether big or small. **-Pastor
Gershon Forde**

As He covers me with His feathers, His love, grace and mercy will
be my portion. When He places me under His wings and gathers me
to Himself, my soul will be satisfied. **-Minister Maria Barrow**

As the hen covers her chicks lovingly with her wings; God will place
his shield lovingly around his children who continue to trust him. **-
Mayleen Gittens**

I think of helpless chickens who constantly need the protection of the mother hen to keep them from danger. We often see the mother hen covering the defenseless chicks with her wings. As helpless beings, we have access to this kind of protection from our loving Father. Once we stay connected to God, we are assured of His protection daily. Trials, testing, and obstacles will arise at some point, but God is your defender and faithful protector. **-Sonia Griffith**

God's word is truth. He stands by it, and we must trust it. It will be all the covering we need. **-Beverly Toppin**

Inductive
BIBLE STUDY

Verse 4:

_____

_____

_____

_____

_____

Examine the verse and make a note of
the words that stand out to you.

Use your concordance to research the words you highlighted
and write their meaning.

_____

_____

_____

_____

Read the verse you're studying in alternate translations. Have
you received any new understanding?

_____

_____

_____

_____

_____

What did the verse mean at the time it was written?

_____

_____

_____

_____

_____

_____

What other scripture/scriptures in the Bible can support this verse?

_____

_____

_____

_____

_____

How can this verse apply to your life?

_____

_____

_____

_____

_____

_____

Additional thoughts?

_____

_____

_____

_____

VERSES 5 & 6

You shall not be afraid of the terror by night, nor of the arrow that flies by day, nor of the pestilence that walks in darkness, nor of the destruction that lays waste at noonday.

Fear. The one word the writer addresses in these two verses. Unfortunately, many people in the body of Christ suffer from fear and anxiety. They love the Lord deeply, but their hearts and minds are filled with uncertainty from the spirit of fear that troubles them daily. They live every day "on edge", always expecting something to go wrong or for something bad to happen. This is not the way God has called us to live.

To any of you who may identify with anything I just said, these two verses are for you. The Lord's promise of protection also extends to your mental and emotional state. He promises that if you are dwelling in Him; you need not fear. Fear is of the enemy, but God offers us life and life more abundantly in all areas. The psalmist tells us we need not be afraid during the day or nighttime. Once we are dwelling in God, we don't have to live in fear, no matter the time of day. **-Pastor Gershon Forde**

As I journey through the night seasons in my life, I will not be afraid of the evil that persists, nor of any danger that lurks, for the Lord my God is my protector. Though I may stumble at times because of the darkness, I can rest assured that my God is always near and will not allow the pestilence to overcome me. He will also remove any and every plan of destruction against my life. **-Minister Maria Barrow**

Whether day or night, the chicks know that once they are in the presence of their mother, there is nothing to be afraid of. We don't need to be afraid. As we go about our day, we must remember that God is in control. **-Mayleen Gittens**

It doesn't matter what time of the day it is; you can always be safe under the wings of the Almighty. As a child growing up, I was afraid of the dark, but in due time, I got to understand God was my protector. My confidence in that protection grew over the years until my faith was cemented in His promises. I recall in my younger years of working having to leave home around 4:30 a.m., to reach my workplace at 5:00 a.m. There were sugar cane fields in front of the house, and on both sides of the road. Some of the employees would always ask if I was not afraid to travel the lonely road. "God is in front of me, Jesus is behind, and the angels are at both sides protecting me." I would always reply. He was my shield, and I was under His wings like a mother hen over her chicks. God was watching over and protecting me, and He can do the same for you. **-Rosalie Weekes**

Calamity can come from any side at any time, but once we find ourselves in the arms of God, it will not destroy us. This doesn't mean we will have a life without pain, but it means that we have a God who will bear us up. **-Beverly Toppin**

Inductive
BIBLE STUDY

Verse 5 & 6:

....

....

....

....

....

Examine the verse and make a note of
the words that stand out to you.

Use your concordance to research the words you highlighted and write their meaning.

_____

_____

_____

_____

Read the verse you're studying in alternate translations. Have you received any new understanding?

_____

_____

_____

_____

_____

What did the verse mean at the time it was written?

_____

_____

_____

_____

_____

What other scripture/scriptures in the Bible can support this verse?

_____

_____

_____

_____

_____

How can this verse apply to your life?

_____

_____

_____

_____

_____

_____

Additional thoughts?

_____

_____

_____

_____

VERSES 7 & 8

A thousand may fall at your side, and ten thousand at your right hand; but it shall not come near you. Only with your eyes shall you look, and see the reward of the wicked.

As I reflected on this verse, I remembered the satellite imagery we see on television during the hurricane season, especially when a hurricane is approaching the island. It is an accepted fact that the eye of the storm is the calmest, because the winds are relatively weaker unlike the rest of the storm. So when the 'eye' is over an area, everything is normally peaceful, however, the surrounding areas are often battered. What came to my mind is this: even when there is a hurricane swirling all around us and likely destroying everything in its path, those who are under God's protection are always in the eye of the hurricane.

We will see the damage that others may experience, but we ourselves will never be destroyed. Yes, at times there will be hurricanes and gale-force winds, storm surges, tropical depressions, and storms, and maybe even the occasional cyclone, but God will be our shelter. Like Paul says in 2 Corinthians 4:8-9, *"We are hard-pressed on every side, yet not crushed; we are perplexed, but not in despair; persecuted, but not forsaken; struck down, but not destroyed."* We can trust and thank the Lord for His promise of protection. **-Pastor Gershon Forde**

Weapons of destruction will fly all around me, but none shall harm me, because God is my strength and shield. When I focus on Him and turn my eyes towards the truth, I will see my enemies fall all around me. Those who want to destroy the work of the Most High, their reward is sure. **-Minister Maria Barrow**

Inductive
BIBLE STUDY

Verse 7 & 8:

_____

_____

_____

_____

_____

Examine the verse and make a note of
the words that stand out to you.

Use your concordance to research the words you highlighted and write their meaning.

_____

_____

_____

_____

Read the verse you're studying in alternate translations. Have you received any new understanding?

_____

_____

_____

_____

_____

What did the verse mean at the time it was written?

_____

_____

_____

_____

_____

_____

What other scripture/scriptures in the Bible can support this verse?

_____

_____

_____

_____

_____

_____

How can this verse apply to your life?

Additional thoughts?

VERSES 9 & 10

Because you have made the Lord, who is my refuge, even the Most High, your dwelling place, no evil shall befall you, nor shall any plague come near your dwelling.

Immediately following all that he says about turbulence, the psalmist returns to the central theme of this verse: dwelling in God's protection. He reminds us that in making the Lord our refuge no evil will befall us, and no plague shall come near our dwelling. I suppose the natural thought that comes to mind is the Israelites in Egypt. No matter how many plagues befell the Egyptians, none of them affected the Israelite household.

The firstborns died in Egypt and yet all the Israelite boys lived. This amazing contrast is something that the psalmist did repeatedly in this psalm as a means of showing us the obvious differences between those who dwell and those who don't. Let me be clear, no part of this psalm is a suggestion that we will float through life with no challenges. Rather, it is a promise that God will be with us as we go through life. **-Pastor Gershon Forde**

Being connected to the vine, the Lord who is my refuge, my strength and my redeemer will keep me safe. Because I am in the will of the Father, no plague will come nigh my home and surroundings. **-Minister Maria Barrow**

God has been my refuge and dwelling place in my times of trials and frustrations. Even though the challenges will come, I want to encourage you to put your confidence in Him. In the story of Job,

God is the one who put a hedge of protection around him. Job didn't and couldn't put up the fortress for himself. Even so, what could a physical fortress do to protect him from the enemy? That hedge of protection over his life was only because of the grace of God. - **Harriette Williams**

Inductive
BIBLE STUDY

Verse 9 & 10:

_____

_____

_____

_____

_____

Examine the verse and make a note of
the words that stand out to you.

Use your concordance to research the words you highlighted
and write their meaning.

_____

_____

_____

_____

Read the verse you're studying in alternate translations. Have
you received any new understanding?

_____

_____

_____

_____

_____

What did the verse mean at the time it was written?

_____

_____

_____

_____

_____

_____

What other scripture/scriptures in the Bible can support this verse?

_____

_____

_____

_____

_____

_____

How can this verse apply to your life?

_____

_____

_____

_____

_____

Additional thoughts?

_____

_____

_____

_____

VERSES 11 & 12

For He shall give His angels charge over you, to keep you in all your ways. In their hands they shall bear you up, lest you dash your foot against a stone.

As if to further illustrate the point that God is our protector, the psalmist then tells us He (God) will give His angels charge (assignment) over us. Their assignment is to keep (protect) us in all our ways and to hold us up before we even hit our foot on a stone. This is a comprehensive promise, but what stands out to me is the attention to detail.

On any day, we may walk and hit our foot on a stone or bump our foot against a chair or something else that is seemingly insignificant. God assures us through these two verses that His promise and His angels are interested in both the big issues of our lives and the ones that we think aren't that important. His promise is without restriction or exception and in this we can be comforted. **-Pastor Gershon Forde**

Verse 11 brings another level of peace to the reader. The author informs us that not only is God committed to protecting us, but He has also commissioned His angels to guard and protect us daily. The next verse is a continuation of said protection. The writer explains that this angelic protection applies to us in such an intimate way that we will not even hit our feet on a stone as we walk around daily. This level of protection is personal. **-Shaniqua Forde**

Inductive
BIBLE STUDY

Verse 11 & 12:

_____

_____

_____

_____

_____

Examine the verse and make a note of
the words that stand out to you.

Use your concordance to research the words you highlighted and write their meaning.

Read the verse you're studying in alternate translations. Have you received any new understanding?

What did the verse mean at the time it was written?

_____

_____

_____

_____

_____

_____

What other scripture/scriptures in the Bible can support this verse?

_____

_____

_____

_____

_____

How can this verse apply to your life?

_____

_____

_____

_____

_____

_____

_____

Additional thoughts?

_____

_____

_____

_____

_____

VERSE 13

You shall tread upon the lion and the cobra, the young lion and the serpent you shall trample underfoot.

This verse reminds me of Mark 16:15-18, where Jesus commissions His disciples and tells them to lay hands on the sick and they shall recover. In Mark, Jesus is speaking to all believers, and in Psalm 91 this verse is written to all who believe; those who dwell in God.

The psalmist lets us know that through our position of dwelling, we can trample upon every serpent and young lion underfoot. Here is the idea: the lions and serpents refer to assignments the enemy has set over our lives to distract, depress, or destroy us.

Regardless of the assignment, God's promise is crystal clear. He will protect us, and we need not fear any enemy. To trample is to showcase authority over a thing, and so we can exercise our authority over the assignments of the enemy because of our dwelling place. - **Pastor Gershon Forde**

Inductive
BIBLE STUDY

Verse 13:

_____

_____

_____

_____

_____

Examine the verse and make a note of
the words that stand out to you.

Use your concordance to research the words you highlighted and write their meaning.

_____

_____

_____

_____

Read the verse you're studying in alternate translations. Have you received any new understanding?

_____

_____

_____

_____

_____

_____

What did the verse mean at the time it was written?

_____

_____

_____

_____

_____

_____

What other scripture/scriptures in the Bible can support this verse?

_____

_____

_____

_____

_____

_____

How can this verse apply to your life?

_____

_____

_____

_____

_____

_____

Additional thoughts?

_____

_____

_____

_____

_____

VERSES 14 & 15

"Because he has set his love upon Me, therefore I will deliver him; I will set him on high, because he has known My name. He shall call upon Me, and I will answer him; I will be with him in trouble; I will deliver him and honor him.

What does it mean to set your love on something or someone? When I think about these two verses, there are two things that stand out to me. In the construction field, one will often hear a mason stating that he has left the cement to "set". What the mason means is that he has applied the cement to the object and is now allowing it to settle in its place. When we hear the term 'setting', it speaks to something not being disturbed or moved.

God, through the psalmist, explains that because we set our love on Him, many promises will follow. Oftentimes our love can be spread around to many people, which is understandable. However, who we love as Master, Savior and Lord, must be God. There can be no wavering or shifting of opinion. We must place every ounce of our love on the Lord. The Bible encourages us not to serve any other gods because to truly serve someone, we must love them. What is the reward for setting our love on God? He promises deliverance and exaltation.

The second thing that comes to my mind is the concept of calling and answering. The psalmist continues in verse 15 to build on the concept of setting our love on God. He says when we call upon God, He will answer us. One of the most annoying things that can ever happen to a child is to call for their mom, dad, or someone else who they trust, and the person does not respond.

Children will repeatedly call a person's name until they answer, and not tire of it because they want to be answered. For the child, answering communicates acknowledgment to them and that is what they are after. In the same way, this verse tells us that when we call on God, He will acknowledge us and respond to our calling. We need not fear whether He cares, or whether He will answer. We can be 100% confident because He will hear and answer us whenever we call. **-Pastor Gershon Forde**

"I will be with him in trouble" The word *"in"* here shows me that the Lord does not always take us out of the storm. If we are saved from everything in life, we will not grow; and our dependency on God will dwindle. So, instead of yanking us from the storm, God sometimes sustains us in the midst of the storm. However, we must continue to hold on to His grace, mercy, peace, and comfort until the battle has ended. **-Ricardo Gittens**

Inductive
BIBLE STUDY

Verse 14 & 15:

_____

_____

_____

_____

_____

Examine the verse and make a note of
the words that stand out to you.

Use your concordance to research the words you highlighted and write their meaning.

_____

_____

_____

_____

Read the verse you're studying in alternate translations. Have you received any new understanding?

_____

_____

_____

_____

_____

_____

What did the verse mean at the time it was written?

_____

_____

_____

_____

_____

_____

What other scripture/scriptures in the Bible can support this verse?

_____

_____

_____

_____

_____

_____

How can this verse apply to your life?

_____

_____

_____

_____

_____

_____

Additional thoughts?

_____

_____

_____

_____

VERSE 16

With long life I will satisfy him, and show him My salvation.

The last verse of this psalm speaks to the duration and quality of life that the dweller is promised by God. The Lord promises He will satisfy us with a long life and show us His salvation. I am especially encouraged by the promise of not just a long life, but a satisfying one. He says He will satisfy us with long life. Could it be that some people may not be satisfied with long life at all? Even though we will age, so long as we stay dwelling, we will be satisfied as we get older. Often, I am blessed by older believers who still have their joy. Despite what they may go through, they can still encourage me whenever we chat.

For me, that is the definition of being satisfied with long life. You are growing older, but the joy of the Lord continues to be your strength. I have no desire to be old and miserable. I want to be satisfied as I age in the Lord. May this be both our prayer and our aspiration as we continue to serve our Lord. The key to it all is clear, dwell in the secret place of the Most High God. **-Pastor Gershon Forde**

Inductive
BIBLE STUDY

Verse 16:

_____

_____

_____

_____

_____

Examine the verse and make a note of
the words that stand out to you.

Use your concordance to research the words you highlighted
and write their meaning.

_____

_____

_____

_____

_____

Read the verse you're studying in alternate translations. Have
you received any new understanding?

_____

_____

_____

_____

_____

_____

_____

What did the verse mean at the time it was written?

_____

_____

_____

_____

_____

_____

What other scripture/scriptures in the Bible can support this verse?

_____

_____

_____

_____

_____

How can this verse apply to your life?

Additional thoughts?

11 Day
DEVOTIONAL

DWELLING IN HIS PRESENCE

He who dwells in the secret place of the Most High Shall abide under the shadow of the Almighty. **Psalm 91:1**

The central word of this verse is *'dwell'*. We should probably discuss what this word means and its importance in our lives. If we dwell in God, we can abide under His shadow. One of the first people to come to mind is David. He spent many hours alone with God because of his professional occupation as a shepherd. Whilst the sheep were at play, David spent his time interacting with the Lord, and it was during this time that he understood the secret dwelling place. When we look at his life, even though not perfect, it proved that He consistently dwelled with God.

> *"Intimacy will not materialize unless quality time is spent."*

God desires a deep, intimate relationship with us, and this can only happen when we dwell. Because the psalmist says, *'secret place'* signifies that even though everyone has access to this place, many will not find it. Why will they not find it? Simply because they do not want to put in the work. **Matthew 7:7** *"Ask and it will be given to you; seek and you will find; knock and the door will be opened to you.*

I can only find something if I search for it. When playing hide & seek, to find the person after the time is up, you must seek them out. Standing there and shouting their name won't help much. You must channel your inner explorer like Dora and go on searching for them. Spending time births intimacy. So if you want to strengthen your relationship with the Lord, it will take dedication.

Remember the Bible says to whom much is given much is required. That intimacy will not materialize unless quality time is involved; and this goes for any relationship. Finding the secret place and being there for a week isn't what this scripture is talking about; consistency is the key. Dwelling is not a onetime encounter; it is conscious daily commitment that will involve sacrifice. Make God your priority and schedule your daily plans around Him. If you want the benefits of the being under His Shadow, you first must dwell.

REFLECTION

Beloved, I want to pose some questions to you, and it is in your best interest that you answer honestly. Are you currently dwelling in the secret place? **YES/NO**

If no, then why?

_____

_____

_____

_____

_____

What steps can you take to get there?

_____

_____

_____

_____

_____

Prayer: Add your prayer for the day and ask God for strength to live out what you would have read.

Declaration: Take the time to write and declare some things over your life pertaining to the topic.

IN HIM, I WILL TRUST

I will say of the Lord, "He is my refuge and my fortress; my God, in Him I will trust."
Psalm 91:2

When you were young, did you ever make this statement? *"I am going to tell my mommy on you; and she will beat you."* And did you do it with your tongue sticking out and the hand on the hip? Without knowing you, I am certain that you would have said something similar when you were a child, at least once.

> *"Trust will require vulnerability and death to self."*

Whenever a child makes this declaration, it is a confidence they have in their parent/guardian to deal with the problem they face. It comes from a place of, *"You are not listening to me now, but I know when my mother comes, she will sort this all out and I will be the winner of this fight."*

This is the same trust the psalmist is expressing in his God. There is no question in his mind about who God is and what He can do. The Lord is his refuge and fortress; and he trusts His ability to fully protect him. In the past, it was hard for me to trust people because of the endless disappointment I endured. Like the times my dad would say he was coming to pick me up but never came. That hurt wrapped around my heart and stood there for many years. When I came to Christ, those trust issues spilled over in my relationship with God, and I found it difficult to trust Him.

My heart knew the Lord could be trusted, but my mind kept going back to the doubt and disappointment. Those trust issues left me crippled to where I looked at everyone through the same negative lens. I felt like they could not be trusted, because trusting people only led to pain. Over the years, as my relationship with the Lord grew, I recognized He could be trusted. He is indeed a man of His word.

Trust will require vulnerability and death to self. **Proverbs 3:5-6** *"Trust in the Lord with all your heart, and lean not on your own understanding."* You must be vulnerable enough to say, *"I have met nothing but disappointment in the past, but that will not stop me from trusting again. Lord, you have proven repeatedly in your word that you will never leave nor forsake. So, I place my unknown future into your hands because you are all-knowing. In you I will trust."* Depending on the trauma from your past, trusting in others may be hard. But I want to let you know God is worthy to be trusted. His word is above His name, so when He says a thing, that it shall be.

REFLECTION

Do you honestly trust the Lord? YES/NO If not, then why?

_____

_____

_____

_____

_____

Dig into scripture and find some people who placed their complete trust in God and show the outcome.

_____

_____

_____

_____

_____

_____

Prayer: Add your prayer for the day and ask God for strength to live out what you would have read.

Declaration: Take the time to write and declare some things over your life pertaining to the topic.

_____

_____

_____

_____

_____

HE SHALL DELIVER ME

Surely He shall deliver you from the snare of the fowler and from the perilous pestilence.
Psalm 91:3

Jehovah Mephalti; the Lord my Deliverer. There is a story in the Bible that we all know well, the parting of the Red Sea. The Israelites were between a rock and a hard place, literally. They stood between the deep sea and the Egyptian army. Out of their helplessness, they cried out and complained.

> *"What you call a 'Giant', is just an uncircumcised Philistine."*

Moses quickly intervened and told them to hold their peace because Jehovah Mephalti would save them. *"And Moses said to the people, "Do not be afraid. Stand still, and see the salvation of the Lord, which He will accomplish for you today. For the Egyptians whom you see today, you shall see again no more forever. The Lord will fight for you, and you shall hold your peace."*
Exodus 14:13-14

The psalmist in Psalm 91: 3 was so confident in God's deliverance that he said, *'surely'*. This word is used to show assurance in something. I'm sure you can underscore many instances in the Bible where God delivered His people. Let me take it a little further and ask you to think about the many times the Lord delivered you from a desolate situation.

The word "deliverer," in Hebrew, means, "to (cause to) escape; to carry away safely" If you are in physical, emotional, mental, or spiritual bondage, I want you to know that there is hope. I sense that some of you have been battling long and hard with those "giants." You have been looking for deliverance from a family member, a friend, a thing, or even yourself.

Listen, that "giant" is just an uncircumcised Philistine, and the best thing about it is, the Lord can deliver you. Just as He heard the groanings of the Israelites, He has heard your cries. There is nothing too big or too small that He can't save you from, so trust in His ability to give you liberty. Don't lose hope now. The God who delivered you then will deliver you now.

REFLECTION

Have you given up hope for your current situation? YES/NO
If no, why?

_____

_____

_____

_____

If yes, why?

_____

_____

_____

_____

How confident are you in God's ability to deliver?

_____

_____

_____

_____

_____

_____

Search for scriptures that show God's deliverance to His people.

_____

_____

_____

_____

_____

_____

_____

Prayer: Add your prayer for the day and ask God for strength to live out what you would have read.

Declaration: Take the time to write and declare some things over your life pertaining to the topic.

_____

_____

_____

_____

_____

HIS TRUTH IS MY SHIELD & BUCKLER

He shall cover you with His feathers, and under His wings you shall take refuge; His truth shall be your shield and buckler. **Psalm 91:4**

The verse says His truth is our shield and buckler. The shield is used as a defensive weapon against the enemy when in a battle. The buckler, which is smaller than the shield, is also used as a defensive weapon in hand-to-hand combat. The psalmist could have used one weapon, but he didn't. This is a perfect example of the protection we receive. God has us covered all around. So, one might ask what *'His truth'* is. It is the word of God. This word can protect us from every attack and fiery dart from the enemy. Can you imagine words being so strong? Well, I can. **Hebrews 4:12** *For the word of God is alive and active. Sharper than any double-edged sword, it penetrates even to dividing soul and spirit, joints and marrow; it judges the thoughts and attitudes of the heart.* There is something powerful about the word of God and it cannot be disputed.

> *"The truth of what God says matters more than the facts you have been presented with."*

When on the battlefield of life, and arrows (Facts) are thrown at us from every corner, we must fight back with His word (Truth). It is your responsibility to refute every lie of the enemy with the truth of God. I have struggled with anxiety from childhood because I listened to Satan's lies. When I understood who I was and what God said about me, I refuted the lies with the word of God. There has been a significant change in my life.

There will be many facts in your life, but you have to decide what the word of God says about them. The doctor has diagnosed you with a disease, that is a fact. But God's word says by His stripes you were already healed. The fact is, you don't have any money and the bill collectors are calling. Here is the truth: Jehovah Jireh is your provider. Do you understand the point I am trying to drive home here? Use the truth of God to defend yourself on this battlefield called life. Don't be moved by what you see, walk in faith, and confess the word of God daily. His truth can move mountains and shift things in your favor.

REFLECTION

Make a list of all the 'facts' you are currently facing.

_____

_____

_____

_____

Make a list of what God says about these things. Consistently confess those truths until you see the evidence. Don't be moved by sight. Continue to walk by faith.

_____

_____

_____

_____

Prayer: Add your prayer for the day and ask God for strength to live out what you would have read.

Declaration: Take the time to write and declare some things over your life pertaining to the topic.

DISPEL THE FEAR

You shall not be afraid of the terror by night, nor of the arrow that flies by day, nor of the pestilence that walks in darkness, nor of the destruction that lays waste at noonday.
Psalm 91:5-6

There is a difference between normal fear and the spirit of fear. Fear is a normal fight/flight response when we encounter danger. The spirit of fear cripples us to such magnitude that it stunts our growth, derails our purpose, and stops us from enjoying life. It seeps into every aspect of our life and

> *"The spirit of fear will strip you of your joy and peace."*

affects everything. The latter type of fear DOES NOT come from the Lord. Where does the spirit of fear come from? It is the workings of Satan to stop us from walking in purpose and living the abundant life God promises. From someone who would have battled with the spirit of fear, I can 'understand' how it takes control of your life. I remember telling my husband one day, "I don't just want to be alive anymore, I want to live." I had been held captive to the chains of fear for so long that it had sucked everything out of me. Even though I was alive, I was not living. I was always thinking negatively and living in constant fear of everyone and everything.

Many people are doing the same thing. They are barely surviving because they are living in daily torment. Walking around like zombies, basically a living dead. You were not called to live in that state of fear. The consequences are not only damaging to you spiritually, but it will also affect you mentally, emotionally, and physically. Imagine being in fight/flight mode every single moment of the day. That is extremely toxic. God is offering you freedom today and every day. Here is some truth for you. If you dwell in the secret place, you will not have to fear. As the verse boldly proclaims, no matter the time of the day, you can walk in the liberty that Christ has given you.

How can you fight against the negativity in your mind? By thinking about the things of God. **Philippians 4:8** *Finally, brethren, whatever things are true, whatever things are noble, whatever things are just, whatever things are pure, whatever things are lovely, whatever things are of good report, if there is any virtue and if there is anything praiseworthy—meditate on these things.* Meditate on the word of God and allow it to transform your mind. When you weed out the bad things, you must always replace them with the right things.

REFLECTION

Are you battling with the spirit of fear? YES/NO If yes, how long have you struggled in this area?

_____

_____

_____

_____

Can you pinpoint where it all started?

_____

_____

_____

_____

What has this fear stopped you from doing?

_____

_____

_____

_____

_____

_____

Search the Bible for scripture relating to fear. Here are a few examples. 1 John 4:18 Psalm 23:4 Psalm 27:1 2 Timothy 1:7.

_____

_____

_____

_____

_____

_____

Prayer: Add your prayer for the day and ask God for strength to live out what you would have read.

Declaration: Take the time to write and declare some things over your life pertaining to the topic.

_____

_____

_____

_____

_____

GOD IS FIGHTING FOR YOU

A thousand may fall at your side, and ten thousand at your right hand; but it shall not come near you. Only with your eyes shall you look, and see the reward of the wicked.
Psalm 91:7-8

In 2 Chronicles 20, the people of Ammon, Moab and Mount Seir were coming fast and furious against the people of Israel. I can picture the fear that was probably raining heavily on the house of Israel. King Jehoshaphat knew that no amount of earthly help could bring them out of the trouble they

> *"Imagine a victory so sweet that you don't even have to lift a finger."*

were facing, so he went to the Lord in prayer. *"O our God, will You not judge them? For we have no power against this great multitude that is coming against us; nor do we know what to do, but our eyes are upon You."* **2 Chronicles 20**. Jehoshaphat was making a bold declaration. His trust was in the Lord to deliver them from the hands of their enemies. Even though he was king, He knew the King of all Kings would be better able to fight the war. So, he humbled himself, used wisdom, and let go of the situation. It was now God's matter to deal with.

The spirit of the Lord came upon Jahaziel and he prophesied, *You will not need to fight in this battle. Position yourselves, stand still and see the salvation of the Lord, who is with you, O Judah and Jerusalem!' Do not fear or be dismayed; tomorrow go out against them, for the Lord is with you."* **2 Chronicles 20:17** These words stood out with me more than anything else, *"for the Lord is with you."* Because king Jehoshaphat knew God personally, the Lord was with him and fought anyone and anything on his behalf. As we see repeatedly, those who commune with God have His protection and guidance.

> *Now when they began to sing and to praise, the Lord set ambushes against the people of Ammon, Moab, and Mount Seir, who had come against Judah; and they were defeated. For the people of Ammon and Moab stood up against the inhabitants of Mount Seir to utterly kill and destroy them. And when they had made an end of the inhabitants of Seir, they helped to destroy one another. So when Judah came to a place overlooking the wilderness, they looked toward the multitude; and there were their dead bodies, fallen on the earth. No one had escaped.* **2 Chronicles 20:22-24**

Isn't this the epitome of, *"a thousand may fall at your side and ten thousand at your right hand but it shall not come near you?"* The people of Israel didn't have to lift a finger, but they could see the destruction of their enemies. Not only did the people of Amon and Moab kill each other, but the people of Israel were blessed in abundance with their spoil. You can find this in verse 25. God broke the backs of their enemies and blessed them at the same time.

Maybe you are asking how this relates to you? Well, God is the same, yesterday, today and forevermore. He is telling you to stand still and see His salvation. You have been fighting too long and hard; it is time to give that situation over to Him and watch it as it all comes together. What have you got to lose? It is time to release control and receive deliverance from your enemies as God has intended.

REFLECTION

Are you a person who likes to be in control? YES/NO If yes, where do you think it stemmed from?

_____

_____

_____

_____

_____

Do you need to have control all the time? YES/NO. If yes, are you ready to let go of the battle and let God fight it for you?

_____

_____

_____

_____

Prayer: Add your prayer for the day and ask God for strength to live out what you would have read.

Declaration: Take the time to write and declare some things over your life pertaining to the topic.

_____

_____

_____

_____

_____

_____

MY REFUGE

Because you have made the Lord, who is my refuge, even the Most High, your dwelling place, no evil shall befall you, nor shall any plague come near your dwelling. **Psalm 91:9-10**.

Have you ever considered a refugee camp? It is a place where people run for asylum and hide from evil. During the holocaust, refugee camps were made for Jews to hide from Hitler and his Nazis. Here is the thing to note; refugee camps only exist where people need protection from oppression. We

> *"The safest place to be in the midst of the battle is under God's shelter."*

are like refugees, seeking a camp of protection from persecution and assaults of the enemy. The Lord is our refuge camp, and even though there is evil, it will not derail us, neither will any plague destroy us. The evil and the plagues exist, but once we are in the camp of God, we are safe.

Refugee camps are temporary. When the threat is gone, there is no longer a need for the camp once everyone gets back to normalcy. With God, however, we have to do the opposite. Making Him our refuge should be a permanent thing. Not only in the valley moments but also when we are on the mountain top. Throughout David's time treading through the wilderness, he found rest, comfort, and shelter in the Lord's refuge camp. He is the ideal example of God being a refuge. In the good, bad, and in between times, he abided.

God is our refuge and strength, a very present help in trouble. Therefore we will not fear, even though the earth be removed, and though the mountains be carried into the midst of the sea; though its waters roar and be troubled, though the mountains shake with its swelling. **Psalm 46:1-3** The palmist mentions many brutal calamities. However, he stands firm by saying that no matter what comes, he will not fear.

REFLECTION

Are you temporarily finding refuge in God, or are you staying there consistently?

_____

_____

_____

_____

If you are dwelling there temporarily, what is hindering you from staying in His presence?

_____

_____

_____

_____

_____

_____

No matter how far you have come there is always more room to grow. If you are dwelling consistently, what else can you do to draw even closer to God?

_____

_____

_____

_____

_____

How are you going to trust God this week to be your refuge?

_____

_____

_____

_____

_____

_____

Prayer: Add your prayer for the day and ask God for strength to live out what you would have read.

Declaration: Take the time to write and declare some things over your life pertaining to the topic.

THE CHARGE!

For He shall give His angels charge over you, to keep you in all your ways. In their hands they shall bear you up, lest you dash your foot against a stone. **Psalm 91:11-12**

What does it mean to give a charge to someone? Whenever a person is installed in a new office, position, job, or otherwise, someone often gives them a charge (a stern admonition) of the dos and don'ts of their new position. Critical to the charge is the person who gives it. They are often in

> *"Isn't it a great feeling knowing that heaven is backing you? You are divinely protected."*

authority over the person being charged. Consider the fact that God has given His angels charge over us. He has explained to them the dos and don'ts of our individual and collective lives. These angels are dispatched on assignment to keep us in check and protect us lest we fall into all the traps the enemy has set forth for us.

The angel of the Lord encamps all around those who fear Him. **Psalm 34:7** Think about the many times we have been saved from death or some kind of evil. Here is a perfect example. A couple of weeks ago, my husband and I went to put gas in the car. As we were waiting on the attendant to complete the credit card transaction, a commotion erupted at the tank next to us. Not knowing the pump was still in the gas tank, a customer turned on the car and started driving off.

The gas attendant immediately yelled at him, and he stopped the car. Everything turned out okay, but it could have ended differently. We both looked at each other and said, "thank you, Jesus." The gas attendant let out a gigantic sigh of relief; as he was shocked by what had happened. This is a perfect example of being spared from danger both known and unknown. This protection is better than any earthly protection. To know that the hosts of heaven are watching over you is such a beautiful thing.

REFLECTION

Have you recently had a "I know that was God watching over me" moment? If so, what was it?

_____

_____

_____

_____

_____

Did you remember to thank God at that moment? YES/NO Even if you did already, take the time to thank Him again.

_____

_____

_____

Take the time to do a list of gratitude. Write out the things you are thankful for today.

Prayer: Add your prayer for the day and ask God for strength to live out what you would have read.

Declaration: Take the time to write and declare some things over your life pertaining to the topic.

TREAD & TRAMPLE

You shall tread upon the lion and the cobra, the young lion and the serpent you shall trample underfoot. **Psalm 91:13**

Whenever we talk about treading, we often think about walking somewhere. As we walk, we tread on the ground. When we speak of trampling, we often think about stomping or mashing something underfoot. The verse in question tells us we will tread upon lions and cobras, and also trample

> *"God has given you authority to tread and trample over the works of the enemy."*

them underfoot. For example, if I were to take a walk across a field, I will naturally tread upon the grass and whatever is in the grass. The act of walking also immediately includes treading upon things like earthworms or other non-threatening insects. However, if I walk across the field and notice a centipede in the grass, my treading will quickly change to trampling, as I immediately appropriate all my force and energy to destroying the centipede. Why? Because the centipede poses a threat to me, whereas the earthworm does not.

The verse above suggests to me that as I am walking through life, the enemy will always be under my feet because of the authority Christ has given me. However, at times when I am walking, I will recognize a threat and straightaway appropriate force. The enemy will always be under our feet, but sometimes we will have to trample him all the same.

Satan never stays dormant forever. He is prone to act up, and when he does, just like the centipede in the field, we must trample him because of the power God has given us. We need not cower in fear or run screaming away from the centipede (Satan). Like David, we must advance towards our Goliath's and trample them in Jesus's name. **Luke 10:19** *Behold, I give you the authority to trample on serpents and scorpions, and over all the power of the enemy, and nothing shall by any means hurt you.*

REFLECTION

Do you honestly believe that you have the power to tread & trample the enemy? YES/NO. If yes, how did you build your confidence in this area?

_____

_____

_____

_____

If no, why?

_____

_____

_____

_____

_____

_____

Here are some tips for developing your confidence:

- Search the Bible for scriptures that show you who you are in Christ. To tread and trample, you first have to understand who you are.

- Repetition is always the key. Daily recite these scriptures until they become a part of you.

- Knowledge is good, but you must always apply it. As the Bible states, faith without works is dead. Now you know who you are, and the authority God has given you, exercise your faith and do what Christ has commissioned you to do. **Mark 16:17-18.**

Prayer: Add your prayer for the day and ask God for strength to live out what you would have read.

Declaration: Take the time to write and declare some things over your life pertaining to the topic.

I WILL BE WITH YOU

Because he has set his love upon Me, therefore I will deliver him; I will set him on high, because he has known My name. He shall call upon Me, and I will answer him; I will be with him in trouble; I will deliver him and honor him. **Psalm 91:14-15**

I love how God says in verse 15, *"I will be with him in trouble"*. One of the most important assurances we can have in life is the knowledge that someone is with us, that they have our back. This is especially comforting when we find ourselves in distressing situations. When we are travel to a new country, go to the doctor, or some other situation, we are often most peaceful when someone is with us whom we love and trust. The word "with" stood out to me when I read verse 15. God is letting us know that no matter what, He will be with us. It's more than knowing He is aware of our situations. It is understanding that God will be right in the middle of everything with us.

> *"The One who calms the raging sea is in the boat with you. Fear not."*

It reminds me of the story in Mark 4:35-41 where Jesus calms the wind and waves. The boat is supposed to cross the sea of Galilee and safely deliver all its occupants to the other side. As the disciples journeyed, a great storm suddenly arises on the sea, and they quickly fear for their lives. To make matters worse, their beloved Jesus, their Rabbi and leader, was not conscious of their turmoil. They found him sleeping in the stern of the boat and felt like he was completely oblivious to all that they were going through.

It is in this distressing moment they awaken Him with a question. *"Master, do you not care that we will perish?"* To put it another way, they were basically saying, *"Jesus, how are you sleeping when we are here fighting for our lives? Don't you care about us?"* I love how Jesus responds to the entire situation. He first rebukes the wind and the waves, and everything immediately calms down. He then he scolds the disciples for forgetting who He was and what that meant.

I believe that just like Jesus' disciples, we often find ourselves in similar situations. It feels as if there's a storm all around, with lots of lightning and thunder, and we feel all alone. Here is the truth: your God will not leave you in a raging storm alone. He has promised to never leave nor forsake us, and in that we can trust. If it feels as if God is asleep and unaware of your calls, be assured that He is in the boat "WITH" you. And because He is by your side, there is no problem, diagnosis, persecution, or turmoil that will ever be too big for Him to intervene and declare "peace be still".

REFLECTION

Have you ever felt as if God was not with you? YES/NO. If yes,
what was the situation?

_____

_____

_____

_____

_____

How did you feel? Were you disappointed, frustrated, angry,
sad, annoyed, abandoned? If none of these adjectives apply, list
your own.

_____

_____

_____

_____

After acknowledging how you felt, what did you do to counteract those negative emotions?

_____

_____

_____

_____

_____

Are you currently going through a storm? Read the quote below and be encouraged.

The way through the turbulent waters of life is not found on a map but by staying close to the one who can navigate and guide us because he himself passed through the greatest storm. -Bob Wenz, 'Navigating Your Perfect Storm'

How has this quote encouraged you?

_____

_____

_____

Prayer: Add your prayer for the day and ask God for strength to live out what you would have read.

Declaration: Take the time to write and declare some things over your life pertaining to the topic.

_____

_____

_____

_____

_____

THE GOD WHO SATISFIES

With long life I will satisfy him, and show him My salvation. **Psalm 91:16**

There are many people who fear old age. Some fear it because they believe that with old age comes sickness and a dependency on others, which makes them uncomfortable. Others fear it because the unknown itself always causes them to be afraid. And there are some who fear old age because there is a

> *"A long and satisfying life comes from the Lord."*

thought that when you become old, you simultaneously become miserable. Hence the statement that many make, "elderly people are just old and miserable." Some elderly people are extremely miserable and that is an unfortunate state to be in at any stage of our lives.

I want to focus on that concept of *'old and miserable'*. One of the greatest promises in this chapter is this last verse. God, through the psalmist declares that with long life, He will satisfy us and show us His salvation. This is such a powerful promise. The Lord is not just saying we will live a long life, but that it will be satisfying.

This scripture isn't only about the quantity of your days, but also the quality of your life. Where one is an estimated amount of a thing, the other is about how excellent that thing is. In Bible times, many of the people lived long, and they were also fruitful even in their old age. Caleb was a great example of this. *As yet I am as strong this day as on the day that Moses sent me; just as my strength was then, so now is my strength for war, both for going out and for coming in.* **Joshua 14:11.** Not only did he live long, but his life was one to be admired, as it beautifully manifested the goodness of the Lord in the land of the living.

Yes, we need to take care of our bodies the best way we know how. However, the longevity to life isn't solely based on diet, exercise, or any other earthly thing you can think of. A long and satisfying comes from the Lord. God offers us satisfaction and salvation in and through Him and it's all connected to the principle which was established from the very beginning. We must first dwell.

REFLECTION

A good way to have a satisfying life is to understand that every season of your life is "your season". Just because it is difficult now doesn't mean it isn't "your season".

Which season are you currently in **SPRING SUMMER FALL WINTER?**

Do some research on the season you chose and see how you can apply the information to your life spiritually.

_____

_____

_____

_____

_____

_____

_____

_____

What things can you do spiritually to make sure you live a satisfying life?

_____

_____

_____

_____

_____

What things can you do physically to make sure you live a satisfying life?

_____

_____

_____

_____

_____

_____

What things can you do mentally to make sure you live a satisfying life?

_____

_____

_____

_____

_____

_____

Find the scripture and fill in the missing spaces by using the NKJV. Before you do, have some fun first by trying to guess it on your own.

_____ is better than life, my lips shall _____ You. Thus I _____ while I live; I will lift up my hands in Your name. My _____ as with marrow and fatness, and _____ shall praise You with joyful lips.

Prayer: Add your prayer for the day and ask God for strength to live out what you would have read.

Declaration: Take the time to write and declare some things over your life pertaining to the topic.

_____

_____

_____

_____

_____

_____

*When you accept the fact that
sometimes seasons are dry and times
are hard and that God is in control
of both, you will discover a sense of
divine refuge, because the hope then
is in God and not in yourself.*

—Charles Swindoll

Made in the USA
Columbia, SC
09 November 2022

70680663R00070